ALPHABEASTS

a hide & seek alphabet book

For Anya,
who helped make it all possible

Library of Congress Cataloging-in-Publication Data
Bernhard, Durga.
Alphabeasts / Durga Bernhard.
p.   cm.
Summary : An alphabetical introduction to the ways
in which real and imaginary animals might use camouflage,
from ape to zebra fish.
ISBN 0-8234-0993-7
1. Animals—Pictorial works—Juvenile literature.
2. Camouflage (Biology)—Pictorial works—Juvenile literature.
3. English language—Alphabet—Juvenile literature.
[1. Animals.   2. Camouflage (Biology)   3. Alphabet.]
I. Title.   II. Title: Alphabeasts.
QL49.B552   1993   92–24980   CIP   AC
591.57′2—dc20
[E]

ALPHABEASTS

a hide & seek alphabet book

by Durga Bernhard

Holiday House / New York

ape

bear

caterpillar

dragon

E

elk

F

frog

goat

H

hummingbird

I

iguana

J

jaguar

K

koala

lioness

monkey

N

newt

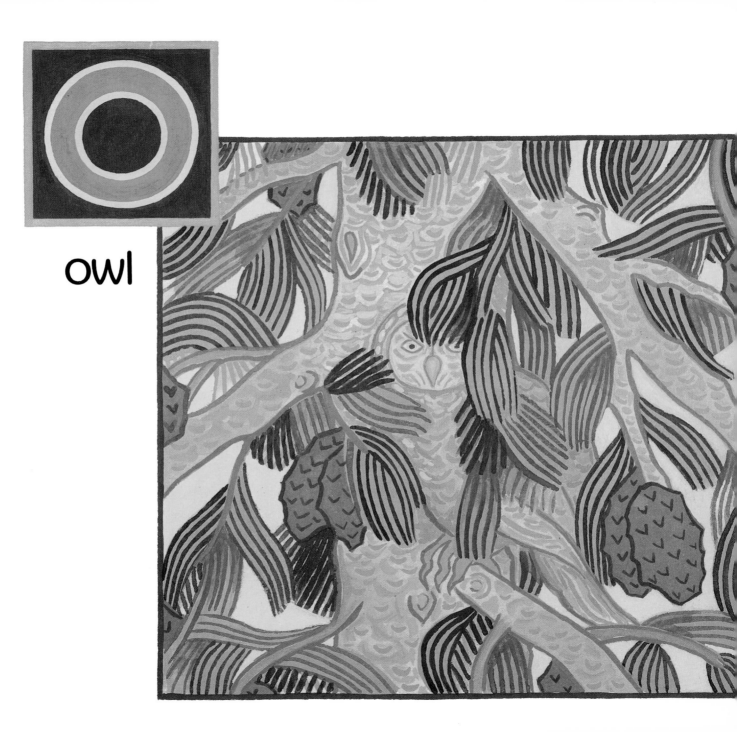

owl

P

porcupine

Q

quail

R

rhinoceros

S

snake

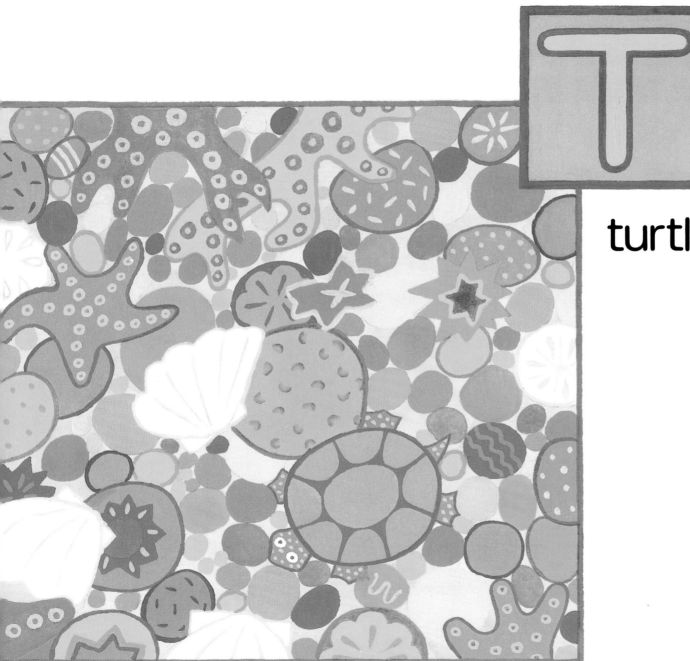

T

turtle

U

unicorn

vicuña

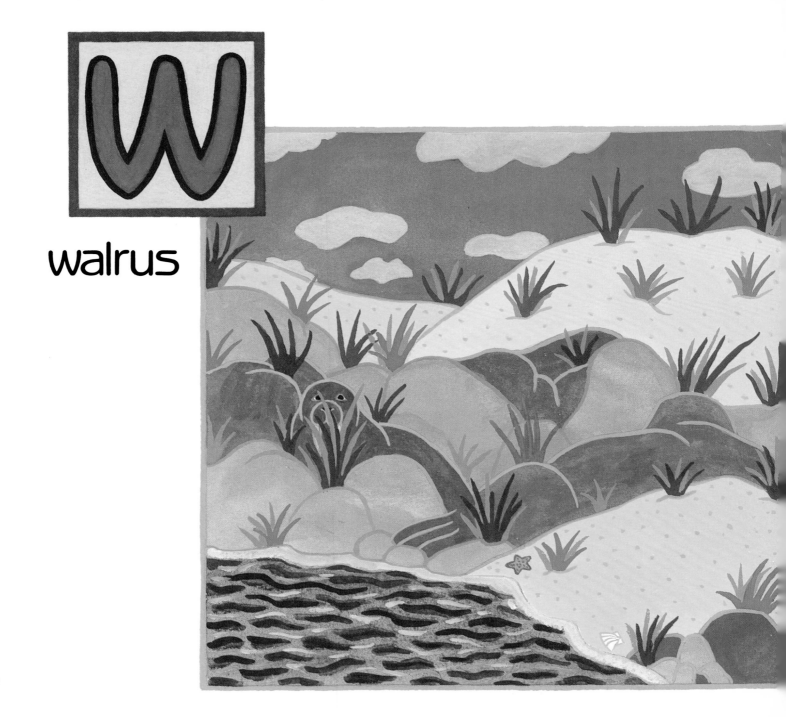

walrus

xenops

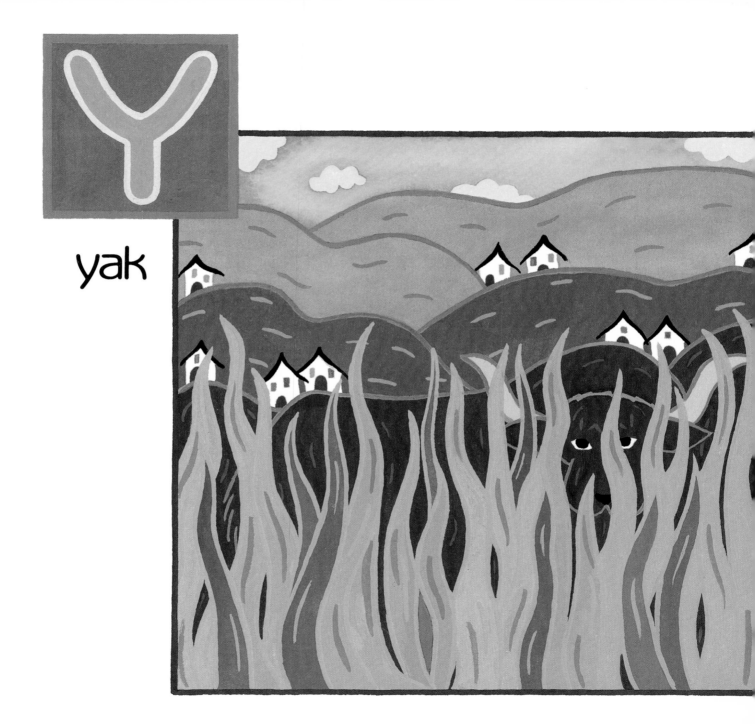

Y

yak

z

zebra fish

Now find ALL the animals.

Now find ALL the letters.